National Museums Scotland

Scottish Explorers

Antony Kamm

SCOTTIES SERIES EDITORS
Frances and Gordon Jarvie

D0784091

Contents

Published in 2013 by
NMS Enterprises Limited – Publishing
a division of NMS Enterprises Limited
National Museums Scotland
Chambers Street, Edinburgh EH1 1JF

Text © Antony Kamm 2013
Images (for © see below)

ISBN: 978–1–905267–43–9

British Library Cataloguing in Publication Data
A catalogue record of this book is available from the British Library.

Book design concept by Redpath.
Cover design by Mark Blackadder.
Layout by NMS Enterprises Ltd – Publishing.
Printed and bound in the United Kingdom by Bell and Bain Ltd, Glasgow.

CREDITS

Thanks are due to the following individuals and organisations who have supplied images and photographs for this publication. Every attempt has been made to contact relevant copyrightholders. If any image has been inadvertently missed, please contact the publisher.

© NATIONAL MUSEUMS SCOTLAND
for pp 2 (map of Arctic); 3 (John Richardson); 4 (John Clark Ross and Ross gull); 5 (*Erebus* and *Terror*); 6 (objects from Franklin expedition, source: *Illustrated London News*); 8 (map of Antarctica); 9 (Bruce expedition and *Discovery* in blizzard); 14 (map of Canada, HBC fort, fur-trappers and sled team, background image); 15 (Alexander Mackenzie); 20 (caravan at Timbuktu, 1853); 22 (James Bruce of Kinnaird, Bruce Nile Cup and background image); 23 (David Livingstone medal and map of Africa); 26 (map of Australia); 32 (Robert Louis Stevenson); 33 (octant and HMS *Challenger* [model]); 35 (David Douglas); 38 (James Tytler and Pilcher's glider); Facts and activities section v (poster); vi (Alexander Dalrymple).

FURTHER CREDITS
(see page viii of 'Facts and Activities section')

SCOTTIE BOOKS

For a full listing of NMS Enterprises Limited – Publishing titles and related merchandise:
www.nms.ac.uk/books

Arctic

An account of Scots who braved the dangerous northern coastlines, icebound islands and frozen seas.

John Ross (1777–1856) was an experienced captain from Wigtownshire who had commanded ships in northern waters. As a young officer he was wounded 13 times in action and had been a prisoner-of-war of the French three times.

The North Pole lies in the middle of the Arctic Ocean, where the sea is 4.3 kilometres deep. On the surface, vast ice floes, sometimes two or three metres thick, grind against each other as they move continually to and fro.

In 1818 two whaling ships with reinforced hulls – *Dorothea* commanded by **David Buchan**, and *Trent* under **John Franklin** – sailed from London.

ARCTIC EXPLORATION 1818-44

A.	Lancaster Sound	G.	Boothia Peninsula
B.	Coppermine River	H.	Melville Island
C.	Fort Enterprise	I.	King William Island
D.	Kent Peninsula	J.	North Magnetic Pole
E.	Mackenzie River	K.	Barrow Point
F.	Prince Regent Inlet	L.	Victoria Island

Their orders were to find a way through the ice at the North Pole and out westward into the Pacific Ocean. After skirting Spitzbergen, they searched for channels through the floes, but ran into packed ice. It took three weeks to extricate themselves and they reported back to the Admiralty that there was no way through.

Also in 1818, a second Admiralty expedition, under **John Ross**, set out through the islands north of Canada in search of the Northwest Passage linking the north Atlantic and Pacific oceans. They sailed through Baffin Bay into Lancaster Sound, but turned back for home after Ross had been deceived by a mirage into thinking that a range of mountains blocked his passage.

In 1819, Franklin returned to the Arctic to explore overland the coast eastwards from the mouth of Coppermine River. His party included **John Richardson**, as surgeon and naturalist, and **John Hepburn**, a courageous seaman who had served on *Trent*. From Fort Enterprise, built as winter quarters, they journeyed by canoe down river, and then explored on foot 500 miles of near impossible terrain. Reaching Kent Peninsula, they were forced by conditions and lack of food to turn back.

John Ross's third winter in Victoria Harbour.

In 1826, Franklin explored the coast westwards from the mouth of Mackenzie River, while Richardson, with two canoes and eleven men, mapped 900 miles of coastline between there and Coppermine River.

The search for the Northwest Passage was resumed in 1829. Ross obtained private sponsorship for a ship, *Victory*, the first steam-powered vessel to explore the Arctic. But while trying to navigate Prince Regent Inlet south from Lancaster Sound, the ship became so stuck in the ice in Victoria Harbour, on the east coast of Boothia Peninsula, that she had to be abandoned.

John Richardson

Sir John Richardson (1787–1865) was born in Dumfries. After studying medicine and natural history at Edinburgh University, he served as a naval surgeon during the Napoleonic wars 1806–14, and was commended for bravery.

In 1821, while returning from the Arctic coast, he was driven to shoot a guide through the head.

The guide had been suspected of murder.

Richardson Mountains and Richardson River are named after him. As a naturalist he gave his name to many discoveries in the animal and plant kingdoms (see pages 34 and vii).

It was a relative of John Ross who now took up the challenge of the Northwest Passage.

James Clark Ross, nephew of John Ross, joined the navy in 1812 when he was only 11. Between 1819 and 1827 he went on four Arctic expeditions. He was in the party which in 1827 failed to reach the North Pole over the ice. In 1829 he was the navy's most experienced active Arctic explorer.

> As well as surveying, James Clark Ross studied and collected specimens of natural phenomena, including the spectacular bird now called Ross's Gull (see below).

In all, the party spent four successive winters in or on the ice, before, in 1833, finding their way safely to another ship in Lancaster Sound. Something had been achieved, however. James Clark Ross explored by sledge Boothia Peninsula (called after the expedition's sponsor, Felix Booth), crossed over the ice what is now called James Ross Strait, and surveyed for the first time coastal areas of what he named King William Land – it was actually an island. He also became the first to discover the North Magnetic Pole, then situated on the west coast of the Boothia Peninsula.

In 1837, **Thomas Simpson**, employee of Hudson's Bay Company, and his colleague **Peter Dease**, mapped the unexplored coast west of the mouth of Mackenzie River. When their boats were stopped by ice, Simpson went on alone, dragging his sledge. He reached Barrow Point, claiming for Britain the land he had discovered on his way. In 1838, the pair fought their way east by boat from the mouth of Coppermine River to Kent Peninsula. Simpson, again on foot, mapped and named Victoria Island. They went even farther in 1839, discovering on the way what

Geographic Poles

The planet Earth has two geographic poles, where the lines of longitude converge. It also has two magnetic poles, to which the compass needle points (north if you are in the northern hemisphere, south in the southern hemisphere). The magnetic poles move around, due to the changing motions of the molten metal in the outer core of Earth which form its magnetic field.

Hudson's Bay Company

Established in 1670 by a royal charter of Charles II, HBC obtained furs from First Nations people in exchange for English goods. Subsequently the company came to control the fur trade throughout British North America. In the earlier part of the 18th century, the company's trappers and other staff were often also explorers.

Sir John Franklin (1786–1847) was a naval officer who surveyed the Arctic region. He died in an attempt to find the route linking the Atlantic and Pacific Oceans.

is now called Simpson Strait. The following year, while returning to Britain via the USA, Simpson was shot in the head in mysterious circumstances.

In May 1845, Franklin sailed again from London in search of the Northwest Passage. His ships, *Erebus* and *Terror*, which had already seen service at the South Pole under James Clark Ross, had been specially equipped with reinforced steel bows, central heating, and a steam engine and screw propeller, to help when there was not enough wind. Each also had a library for recreational reading. In port at Greenland, provisions for three years were loaded on board, including 8000 tins of cooked or preserved meat and soup, to feed the 129 officers and men,

among whom it is believed there were several Scots. The last sighting of the two ships, however, was in Baffin Bay.

Erebus and *Terror*

Franklin's ships were converted bomb ships with three masts, originally designed to carry, and withstand the recoil from, two three-ton mortars. They were stronger than a normal vessel, but ponderous to manœuvre under sail. In 1842, returning to the Falkland Islands for the winter, the ships collided while avoiding an iceberg. Disaster was averted by Ross's coolness and nautical skills. After his expedition, *Erebus* and *Terror* were refitted for Franklin's last voyage to the Arctic.

The mysterious fate of Franklin and his men continued to haunt those who explored the far reaches of the Arctic.

Among the first to realise that something might be wrong with the Franklin expedition was **William Penny**, a whaler operating out of Cumberland Sound. In 1847, and again in 1849, he tried unsuccessfully to sail through Lancaster Sound. In the meantime the Admiralty had sent out search expeditions under James Clark Ross (by sea) and John Richardson (overland). Another expedition, under John Ross, financed by private sponsorship, public subscription and his own money, sailed in 1850. Between then and 1880, 25 further expeditions were mounted, and the search for the two ships, by sonar and magnetonic methods, is still going on today.

The expeditions discovered that *Erebus* and *Terror* had been encased in the ice off King William Island, and evidence suggested that Franklin had died in June 1847.

Background: Items from the Franklin expedition, including part of a compass, forks, spoons and buttons, sold to John Rae by Inuit people.

John Rae

Rae (1813–93), born in Orkney, was one of the greatest Arctic overland explorers, and a good friend of the First Nations people, from whom he learned methods of survival and living off the land.

A qualified surgeon, Rae was employed by the Hudson's Bay Company (1833–56), becoming chief factor (regional manager and member of the governing council) in 1850. During his four expeditions, he travelled 10,000 miles on foot or by small boat, and surveyed 1800 miles of coast. Within only 35 years, three Scots – James Clark Ross, Thomas Simpson and John Rae – mapped the entire Canadian Arctic coastline.

During the following winter 26 of his men also died. Modern scientists have concluded that they suffered from scurvy, tuberculosis, and lead poisoning from the sealant of the tins of meat. By April 1848, the men appeared to have decided to abandon the ships to try to reach the mainland on foot and by lifeboat. Not a single man survived.

It was 1854 before there was any definite news of the expedition's fate. **John Rae**, on his fourth exploration of the Arctic, encountered Inuit people who described ships frozen in the ice, and men dying from starvation as they struggled unsuccessfully to pull their sledges to safety. They also sold items to Rae which could only have come from Franklin's expedition (see opposite). Rae brought the devastating news back to England, and in 1856, after some controversy, he and his men were given the £10,000 reward for definite news of the expedition's fate.

In 1929, the Norwegian **Roald Amundsen** became the first to sail through the North-west Passage. The first party to reach the geographical North Pole on foot was led by **Sir Wally Herbert** in 1969. In between these two achievements, in 1934, a three-man expedition under an army officer, **Martin Lindsay**, secured another first. They crossed Greenland from west to east, travelling 1080 miles in 103 days and setting a record for a self-supporting journey by dog-sledge. On the way, 700 miles of which was over new ground, they travelled across the Greenland ice-cap, which rises to 3310 metres, and mapped 350 miles of mountainous country along the east coast.

Lindsay with huskies and sledge in 1930–31, when he was surveyor to the British Arctic air-route expedition.

Arctic first

Margaret Penny, from Aberdeen, wife of William Penny, was the first Scottish woman in the Arctic. In 1857 she accompanied her husband on a winter whaling expedition to Baffin Island. She wrote an account of her life there, describing the Inuits, with whom she maintained close contact.

Doomed!

Among the 16 out of 24 members of the badly-equipped and ill-prepared Canadian Arctic Expedition (1913–14) who died or disappeared were Scots **Alexander Anderson** (first officer), **Alistair Forbes Mackay** (surgeon) and **James Murray** (biologist). **William Laird McKinlay** (meteorologist), **John Munro** (chief engineer), and **Robert Templeman** (cook) survived. Their ship, *Karluk*, was trapped in the ice off the north coast of Alaska and drifted erratically several hundred miles west, before being crushed and sinking off Wrangel Island. The survivors were finally saved after their captain walked 700 miles over the frozen Chukchi Sea and across Siberia to mount a rescue operation from Alaska.

Antarctic

Scots who explored the glacial coasts and inlets, studied the environment, reached the South Pole, and tried to cross the continent itself.

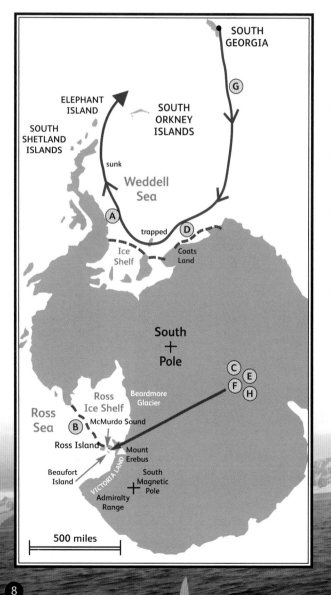

James Weddell taught himself navigation while in the navy. His Antarctic explorations were sponsored by Messrs Strachan and Grant of Leith, near Edinburgh.

The name of Franklin recalls adventure and tragedy in the Arctic. For the same reasons, we associate the exploits of **Scott** and **Shackleton** (1901–16) with the windswept, frozen land mass (half as big again as Australia) and the ice-packed seas surrounding it at the South Pole. Scottish interest, however, began earlier.

Between 1819 and 1824, **James Weddell** made three voyages to the Antarctic in search of seals. He mapped the South Shetland and the South Orkney Islands. He discovered a new sea, later named Weddell Sea, through which he sailed to latitude 74°15', the most southerly point reached up until that time.

ANTARCTIC		
A. Weddell		1822–24
B. Clark Ross		1839–43
C. Scott	Discovery	1901–04 ←
D. Bruce	Scotia	1902–04
E. Shackleton	Nimrod	1907–09 ←
F. Scott	Terra Nova	1910–13 ←
G. Shackleton	Endurance	1914–16
H. Mackintosh	Aurora	1914–17 ←

During a voyage of exploration and scientific discovery in 1839–43, **James Clark Ross** (see also pp. 4, 5 and 6) and the crews of the *Erebus* and *Terror* were the first to see and name Victoria Land, the Admiralty range of mountains, and the active volcano Mount Erebus. They too were the first to brave the hazards of what became known as the Ross Sea, and the Ross Ice Shelf, an impenetrable mass of solid ice twice the size of the United Kingdom, whose cliff face rises in places 50 metres above the level of the sea.

The British National Antarctic (or Discovery) Expedition (1901–04) was led by Commander (later Captain) **Robert Falcon Scott**, with Scotland-born Lieutenant Albert Armitage as second-in-command, and Ernest Shackleton as a junior officer. Many trips were made from the base set-up at McMurdo Sound to explore the region and conduct scientific experiments. A team attempt, however, to reach the South Pole failed, 480 miles from its goal.

In November 1902, *Scotia* sailed for the Antarctic from Troon on a scientific expedition. Its leader and inspiration was **William Speirs Bruce**. Bruce was a polar scientist who already had practical experience in the Arctic in 1896–97, on an expedition where Armitage was also a member, and again in 1898–99.

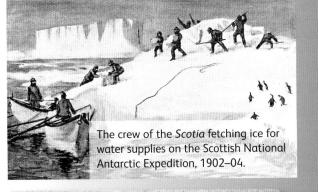

The crew of the *Scotia* fetching ice for water supplies on the Scottish National Antarctic Expedition, 1902–04.

William Speirs Bruce

In 1902, Bruce (1867–1921) led the Scottish National Antarctic Expedition, sailing from Troon aboard the *Scotia*. Read about his explorations at:

www.south-pole.com/p0000093.htm

www.undiscoveredscotland.co.uk/ usbiography/b/williamspeirsbruce.html

archiveshub.ac.uk/features/jan03.shtml

Scotia, a steam yacht, 42.7 metres long and 8.8 metres across, was rebuilt and equipped in Troon specifically for the expedition. Her entire crew of 27 officers and men was Scottish, as were most of the six scientific staff.

The expedition came home in 1904, having discovered the coastline which they named Coats Land (after its main sponsors) and bearing extensive collections of scientific specimens and valuable data.

Discovery was a wooden sailing ship, purpose-built in Dundee, a former major whaling centre. She has returned to her home town and can be visited. Go to **www.rrsdiscovery.com** to find out more.

Ernest Shackleton returned to the Antarctic in 1907–09 for another crack at the South Pole.

His ship, *Nimrod*, was a 40-year-old wooden-hulled sealing vessel with a single propeller, longer, but narrower and lighter even than *Erebus*. Among the crew were Scots second officer **Aeneas Mackintosh**, who lost an eye in an accident soon after arrival, and **James Paton**, seaman. Members of the shore party included **Alistair Forbes Mackay**, assistant surgeon, and **James Murray**, biologist (see page 7), in charge of the base camp on Ross Island during the attempt on the South Pole.

Shackleton and a three-man team were forced to turn back 97 miles from the Pole.

Other assignments, however, including the collection of geological specimens, were successful. Mackay was one of the squad which scaled Mount Erebus (4023 metres) for the first time. Several months later, he and two others travelled 1260 miles on foot, dragging their sledges, to reach the South Magnetic Pole, where they raised the Union Jack and gave three cheers for King Edward VII.

Terra Nova took **Scott**'s expedition of 1910–13 to the Antarctic. Once again, the principal aim was to reach the Pole, using Siberian ponies to pull the sledges.

Only when they arrived at McMurdo Sound did they learn that the Norwegian Roald Amundsen had landed farther along the Ross Ice Shelf, and that he too was planning a journey to the Pole.

Ernest Shackleton

Ernest Shackleton (1874–1922) was an Anglo-Irish explorer and merchant seaman, who became secretary of the Scottish Royal Geographical Society. He sailed to the Antarctic on *Discovery* in 1901, and led his own expeditions in 1908, 1911 and 1915. Early in 1915, his ship *Endurance* became trapped and crushed in the polar ice. Shackleton's amazing leadership and courage ensured the survival of his crew. On a fourth expedition in 1922, he died of a heart attack and was buried in South Georgia.

Shackleton's Boat Journey, by *Endurance*'s skipper Frank A. Worsley, is a famous account of the third expedition.

Gathering in the main sail of the *Terra Nova* in the pack ice, 1910. James Paton, who was on the *Nimrod*, was one of the seamen on this trip too.

On 1 November 1911, twelve men, with ponies and sledges, left base camp. One by one the ponies foundered in the snow and ice, and had to be shot. Then it was every man pulling, while supplies for the return journey were dropped off. On 20 December, as had been planned, four men turned back and headed for base.

On 6 January 1912, barely 100 miles from the Pole, Scott decided to press on for the final lap with a team of five, not four, as had been planned. The fifth man was the Scot **Henry Bowers** (seated, left) who was chosen for his efficiency, powers of endurance and his navigational skills.

On 16 January, as they approached the Pole, it was he who spotted the runner of a sledge stuck in the snow, with a black flag tied to it. Amundsen had got there first!

Above: Scott's party at the Pole, bitterly disappointed by Admunsen's success.

Left: The team of the *Terra Nova* expedition pulling a sled on their way to the South Pole.

Neither Scott nor any of his four companions survived the final journey.

The last three, Scott, Bowers and **Edward Wilson** the expedition's doctor, died in their tent around 30 March, 11 miles from the next depot. Their bodies were found nine months later.

With the race to the South Pole now lost, Shackleton embarked on an even more ambitious project – to cross the whole continent from the Weddell to the Ross seas, via the Pole. The crossing itself never even began, but the trans-Antarctica Expedition 1914–17 still became a legend. Two ships were involved.

Endurance would land the trans-Antarctic party and scientists at the Weddell Sea.

Aurora would go to the Ross Sea, from which its crew would lay depots from the coast to the Pole for the second part of the journey.

With *Endurance* were Scots **James Wordie**, geologist and chief scientist, **Robert Clark**, biologist (above, in his laboratory on board), **Harry McNish**, the ship's carpenter, known from his calling as 'Mr Chippy', and **Thomas McLeod**, seaman. *Aurora* was commanded by Aeneas Mackintosh, with the ever-present Paton as boatswain.

Mrs Chippy

Mrs Chippy, the cat aboard *Endurance* – pictured here with Perce Blackborow (a stowaway and youngest member of the crew) – was actually a male. He was looked after by Harry McNish. McNish never forgave Shackleton for having Mrs Chippy shot when *Endurance* was abandoned, on the grounds that the sled dogs would tear the cat to pieces.

Endurance struggled through the Weddell Sea until the ice closed in, with only 100 miles to go. Then for nine months the ship drifted out of control, gripped by the ice. When the hull became crushed beyond hope of repair, Shackleton ordered the crew to abandon ship and set up camp on the shifting ice.

For five months the 28 men survived precariously as they tried to reach land. As the ice began to break up, they took to the three lifeboats they had hauled along with them.

In April 1916 they landed on the remote and uninhabited Elephant Island. But as it was not known they were there, no one would come to their rescue.

Endurance, almost the end.

'Like semi-frozen sardines ...'

Two lifeboats were upturned, lashed together, and lagged against the conditions to make the Snuggery. Twenty-two men lived and slept there, packed 'like semi-frozen sardines'.

The nearest inhabited place was the whaling station on South Georgia, off Cape Horn, nearly 800 miles away across the most notorious seas in the world. Shackleton had the third lifeboat refurbished and strengthened by McNish, one of the six-man crew who set out in April 1916 to bring help.

The impossible journey, with a sail and oars, and rudimentary navigational instruments, took 16 days, through seas higher than Shackleton had ever seen. They finally landed on the wrong side of the island. Shackleton crossed previously unclimbed and unmapped mountains on foot, to raise the alarm.

Three international attempts to reach Elephant Island failed. But on 30 August 1916, a Chilean steamer, with Shackleton on board, reached the trapped men. All had survived.

Aurora, on the other side of the continent, was blown out to sea in 1915, leaving the shore party of ten under Mackintosh without support. Somehow, over the next six months in appalling conditions, they managed to lay a trail of depots across the ice shelf as far as the Beardmore Glacier. Then, unable to reach their base at Cape Evans on Ross Island, they settled in temporary quarters. In May 1916, concerned that the party might miss the return of *Aurora*, Mackintosh and a companion set out for Cape Evans over the breaking ice. They were never seen again.

Canada

Scots who ventured into the unknown, forged trade routes, and linked new communities across some of the most difficult terrain in the world.

Above: Hudson's Bay fur trappers form a dog-train, with drivers running alongside the teams.

Left: A fort belonging to the Hudson's Bay Company, late 19th century.

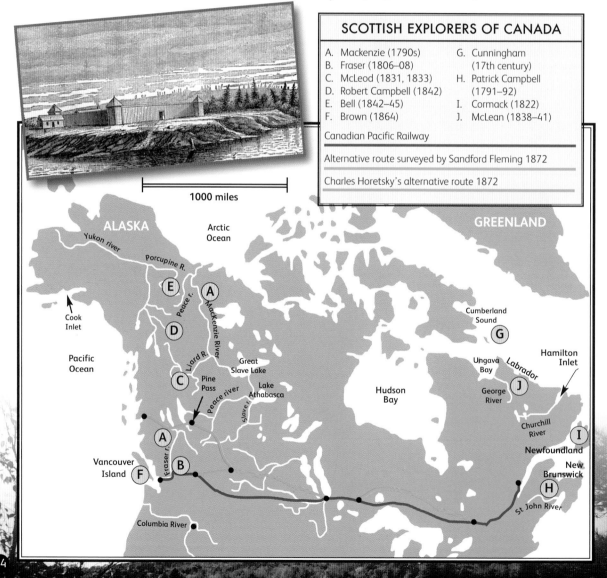

SCOTTISH EXPLORERS OF CANADA

A. Mackenzie (1790s)
B. Fraser (1806–08)
C. McLeod (1831, 1833)
D. Robert Campbell (1842)
E. Bell (1842–45)
F. Brown (1864)
G. Cunningham (17th century)
H. Patrick Campbell (1791–92)
I. Cormack (1822)
J. McLean (1838–41)

Canadian Pacific Railway

Alternative route surveyed by Sandford Fleming 1872

Charles Horetsky's alternative route 1872

1000 miles

ALASKA
Arctic Ocean
GREENLAND
Yukon river
Porcupine R.
Cook Inlet
Pacific Ocean
Peace r.
Mackenzie River
E
A
D
Liard R.
C
Pine Pass
Peace river
Great Slave Lake
Lake Athabasca
Slave r.
Cumberland Sound
G
Hamilton Inlet
Ungava Bay
Labrador
J
George River
Hudson Bay
Churchill River
I
Newfoundland
A
Fraser r.
B
Vancouver Island
F
New Brunswick
H
St. John River
Columbia River

Many Scottish-Canadian explorers were involved in the fur trade, with North West Company (NWC), or with Hudson's Bay Company (HBC, which merged with NWC in 1821). When a Canadian border was created in 1783, merchants looked to expand their business in the north west and open up trade links across the Pacific Ocean. **Alexander Mackenzie** (NWC) was charged with discovering a route which could be used for transport from Great Slave Lake to the Pacific.

The mouth of the great river which flowed out of the lake to the west (later named after him) was thought to be at Cook Inlet in Alaska. Mackenzie's party negotiated by canoe the difficult passage via Slave River from the company's base on Lake Athabasca into Great Slave Lake. They then started the descent of the river, which flowed west, then north.

After following it for 1075 miles, they found themselves in the Arctic Ocean! The outward journey had taken two weeks. Travelling back against the current took two months.

Mackenzie decided that next time he would be better prepared, with instruments to find out his exact position. In 1793 he set out up Peace River to its source in the mountains, hoping from there to find a river which flowed west. The going became so tough that some of his boatmen begged him to give up.

Finally, after further travel upstream, numerous portages (carrying canoes across land), going back on his tracks because of impossible water, and meetings with friendly, and not so friendly, natives, he found a way to the Pacific coast at the mouth of Bella Coola River, north of Vancouver Island. The return journey was done in two months, an average of 25 miles a day on foot carrying canoes and equipment, and 36 miles a day (including portages) in turbulent rivers. In all, he travelled 2300 miles.

Sir Alexander Mackenzie

At the age of 48, Alexander Mackenzie (1764–1820) retired from the fur trade and came back to Scotland, where he married 14-year-old Geddes Mackenzie. She and her twin sister had inherited the estate of Avoch, Ross-shire. He bought it from them and lived there with Geddes. Mackenzie died at an inn near Dunkeld while returning from a visit to a doctor in Edinburgh.

The 'impossible water' that Mackenzie encountered is now called Fraser River, then thought to be the Columbia. **Simon Fraser** (NWC) was handed the dangerous task of following it to the sea. In 1808, his 24-man party, with **John Stuart** as second-in-command and navigator, left Fort George in four canoes. Thirty-six days later, after braving whirlpools and rapids, and lugging their canoes overland where the way was utterly impassable, they reached the river's mouth. It was not the mouth of the Columbia, nor could they see the open ocean; that was 140 miles farther on, across Vancouver Island. Adding to these disappointments, the NWC then decided that the Fraser River route was no more practical for its purposes than Mackenzie's.

Simon Fraser

Simon Fraser (1776–1862), a fur trader, built a fort in 1807 – Fort George (now Prince George) – where Nechako River flows into Fraser River near its northernmost point. It was a NWC post. He called the area New Caledonia.

Scottish employees of HBC undertook further exploration in the west. In 1834, **John M. McLeod** followed the western branch of Liard River to its source, covering 311 miles of unknown territory.

In 1840, **Robert Campbell** (HBC) was instructed to continue McLeod's explorations, this time along the northern branch of the Liard system. He pressed on to Pelly River, and in 1842 descended it to where it joined another big river, which he called the Lewes (now Yukon). From there, in 1851, he examined the route to Fort Yukon, where Porcupine River joins the Yukon.

John Bell (HBC) explored Peel River from where it flows into the Mackenzie, and in 1845 crossed over west to Porcupine River. He thus opened up for the company an easier route to the Yukon than the one discovered by Robert Campbell.

Robert Brown from Caithness was a botanist, sponsored by the British Columbia Botanical Association of Edinburgh to collect seeds. The association, however, was unimpressed by the seeds he sent back from his expedition to Vancouver Island in 1863. The next year he accepted the post of commander of the Vancouver Island Exploring Expedition. Altogether, the three groups comprising the expedition covered 1200 miles, mapping the region and establishing place names. His seeds, however, were still regarded as unsatisfactory.

In 1605, **John Cunningham**, a naval officer employed by the king of Denmark, landed on the east coast of Greenland. He and his crew explored and mapped the immediate area, and returned with mineral samples and several kidnapped Inuit, who were put on display in Copenhagen. As part of a larger expedition the following year, he sailed along the coast of Labrador, almost to Cumberland Sound.

Patrick Campbell travelled with his dog to North America in 1791, on his own initiative, to investigate the conditions for immigrating Highlanders. To do this, he made the difficult journey up St John River, New Brunswick, and then overland to the St Lawrence.

William Eppes Cormack became in 1822 the first European to explore the interior of Newfoundland. With a companion he crossed the island from east to west on foot, negotiating vast prairies dotted with lakes. As he travelled, Cormack recorded details of the weather conditions, soil, flora and fauna.

John McLean was in charge of the HBC district centred on Ungava Bay, Labrador. In 1839, determined to find a practical route from there to the base at Hamilton inlet, he and his crew started up George River, then travelled overland to the head of Churchill River, where he was the first European to see the Churchill Falls. The next year he found a way round the Falls and established the internal link.

Canadian Pacific Railway

This image records the completion in 1885 of the Canadian Pacific Railway, built initially in return for the province of British Columbia on the Pacific sea coast joining the new Dominion of Canada. **Donald A. Smith**, a director of CPR, hammers in a ceremonial last spike. Behind his right shoulder is the imposing figure of **Sandford Fleming**, the engineer who in 1872 headed the expedition which explored a possible route from ocean to ocean. Also on this epic journey were **George Monro Grant**, expedition secretary, and **Charles Horetzky**, photographer, who investigated an alternative passage to the Pacific via Pine Pass.

Africa

In London in 1778, 12 Britons, including 6 Scots, formed the African Association to promote trade with Africa and discover more about its geography.

In 1794, a 23-year-old Scot from near Selkirk volunteered his services to the African Association. **Mungo Park** had recently been ship's doctor on a voyage to Sumatra, during which he discovered several new species of fish. He was taken on to explore the course of the Niger. In December 1795, he set out on horseback from Pisania in Gambia, with two African servants, having in the meantime learned the local language so that he could speak to people without an interpreter. His clothes were what a doctor in Scotland would wear: thick breeches fastened below the knee, heavy bright blue coat with gilt buttons, and a tall hat, in which he hid the notes he made during his journey.

The going was painfully slow, but in spite of the heat Park assiduously kept up his journal. At Kemmoo he was forced to make a detour to the north east to avoid tribal warfare. Then he was captured by Moors (Muslims of part Arab, part Black African descent), who treated him cruelly and humiliated him for being Christian.

SCOTTISH EXPLORERS IN NORTHERN AND WESTERN AFRICA

Bruce (1770)	Laing (1825/26)
Park (1795–97)	Baikie (1854/57)
Park (1805)	
Clapperton/Oudney (1822–24)	
Clapperton (with Lander) (1825–27)	

Background image: A view of Kamalia, drawn from Park's own sketch in his notebook.

Mungo Park

Mungo Park (1771–1806) had enormous energy. One night on his second expedition, he crossed and recrossed a crocodile-infested river 16 times, carrying men and loads (after which he admitted to feeling 'some-what fatigued')! Though he observed, and experienced, the horrors of the slave trade, he said very little about it publicly.

After three months Park escaped. Weak from hunger, thirst and fever, he continued his journey alone. At Segu he finally saw the majestic Niger flowing eastward and followed its course on foot for 75 miles. At Silla, exhausted, sick and plagued by mosquitoes and the rains, he reluctantly decided he must turn back.

Park stumbled along the way for 300 miles, begging for his food. At Kamalia he collapsed from fever. A slave-trader cared for him until the rains had ceased. Then, along with a company of slaves who were being taken to Gambia, he set off again for Pisania, where he was greeted by people who thought he was dead. With no ship to Britain due, he joined a slave-ship bound for America. From Antigua, he took a mailboat to England. He had been away for two years, seven months, but he still had his hat, and his journal.

Eight years later, Park returned to Pisania to continue exploring the Niger. He had with him 44 Europeans, including two Scots (his brother-in-law **Alexander Anderson**, and **George Scott**, as artist), soldiers from the Royal Africa Corps, and carpenters to build a ship to sail down river. Four months later, when he reached the Niger's immense, rolling waters, he had only 12 people left. Rains, heat and fever had taken their toll.

Scott had died on the way. Anderson died at Sansanding, where Park himself, with one soldier, constructed a rudimentary boat out of two rotten, leaking canoes. Now left with four survivors of his original party, one of them a crazed soldier, he sailed for 1500 miles, with hostile tribes on either bank, to find out where the Niger went. At Bussa, where the river narrows and gives way to fearsome rapids, the boat was trapped by rocks. Nobody really knows what happened next. Park and his crew were either attacked and killed by mobs from above, or drowned in the raging waters.

In 1827, Park's son Thomas, a naval officer, tried to find his father, believing him still to be alive. After writing to his mother from the Gold Coast, Thomas was never heard from again.

Still no one knew where the mighty Niger arrived at the ocean.

In 1822, two Scots, **Hugh Clapperton** and **Walter Oudney**, both naval officers, and an Englishman, **Dixon Denham**, set out across the Sahara desert by the trade route from Tripoli. Their assignment was to discover whether the Niger flowed into Lake Chad.

They were the first Europeans to find the lake, but it did not provide the answer to their search. Clapperton and Oudney went on to discover River Shari, and prove that it was not the Niger. They then turned west-ward, towards Kano and the Niger itself. On the way Oudney died of pneumonia. Clapperton went on to Kano and the king-dom of Sokoto, to whose rulers he offered trade with Britain if they would give up dealing in slaves.

Clapperton (above) returned to Britain in 1825, convinced that the mouth of the Niger lay in the Bight of Benin. Though in poor health, he persuaded the British Colonial Office to send him straight back to Africa. His brief was to establish good relations with the rulers of Sokoto, persuade them to

Annan-born Hugh Clapperton (1788–1827) was press-ganged into the Royal Navy as a teenager. Before joining Oudney in 1822, he fought as a lieutenant in the Napoleonic Wars.

renounce the slave trade, and establish the course of the Niger.

In November 1825, Clapperton set out from Badagri on the coast. He was accompanied by three officers, all of whom died within the first few weeks, and by his Cornish servant, **Richard Lander**. At Bussa, Clapperton carried a sick Lander across streams that his servant was too weak to swim. They went on to Kano and Sokoto, where Clapperton himself died, of dysentery, in Lander's arms.

A caravan approaches Timbuktu in 1853.

In the meantime, the search for the course of the Niger had become a race. In 1822, another Scot, **Alexander Laing**, had seen from a distance the land where the river rose and calculated that it could not flow into the River Nile, as some still thought.

In July 1825, he left Tripoli for the lower reaches of the Niger. In August 1826, after a hair-raising journey of 2650 miles across the desert, he became the first European to enter Timbuktu. He was allowed to stay there for several weeks, only to be killed outside its walls when he tried to move on.

It was Richard Lander, with his brother **John**, who in 1830, by sailing down the Niger from Bussa in two canoes, finally proved that Clapperton was right about where it ended.

Timbuktu

Leo Africanus, a Muslim traveller, visited the city of Timbuktu in about 1510. He reported on the magnificence of the royal court, and the military might which attended the king, who paid the living expenses of priests, judges, scholars and doctors. In the shops, European goods were sold and books were the most sought-after merchandise. Even though by the end of the 18th century these reports of wealth and learning no longer applied, the mystery of Timbuktu lingered.

Alexander Laing

While Clapperton and Oudney were modest and careful, Laing (1792–1826) was more arrogant and conceited. In the same way as Park, however, he was brave, determined and indifferent to risk. In Tripoli, he fell in love with the daughter of the British consul-general. They were married, much to her father's dismay, four days before the start of the expedition. On the journey, the caravan which his party joined at In Salah was attacked by Tuareg nomads. Laing was shot, and slashed with sabre cuts to his head, neck, arms and hands, but somehow survived.

In 1854, **William Baikie**, a naval surgeon from Orkney, sailed up the Niger from its mouth in a steamer, to investigate the establishment of a trading settlement in the interior. Baikie also produced scientific data on 700 miles of the rivers Niger and Benue. For protection against the dreaded malaria, he prescribed quinine for his crew. Not a man died on the 16-week voyage.

In 1857, Baikie commanded a second expedition, in the steamer *Day Spring*, to set up trading posts and make geological surveys. It came to grief at the Bussa rapids, where his ship was wrecked. A rescue party reached them a year later, but Baikie stayed on. He bought land and built a settlement at Lokoja, made the Niger more navigable, and constructed roads. Ordered home for health reasons in 1864, he died on the way, in Sierra Leone ('the White Man's Grave')
.

Geographers had wondered about the source of River Nile since the second century AD.

The Scottish adventurer **James Bruce of Kinnaird** thought he had discovered it in 1770, on the southern shore of Lake Tana. It was in fact the Blue Nile, which runs into the Nile itself. In the course of a remarkable journey, he travelled 2000 miles overland from Massawa on the Red Sea to Cairo, recording with care everything he saw.

Bruce and his companions took three months to cross the mountain barriers between Massawa and Gondar. There and later he was caught up in local wars and disputes from which he managed to extricate himself by demonstrations of horsemanship, shooting and medical skills. His party spent 22 terrible days crossing 400 miles of desert between Chendi and Aswan, having killed, and eaten, the last of their camels.

David Livingstone, Scottish missionary and doctor, tried, and failed, to identify the source of the Nile, but during many lengthy, exhausting expeditions over 31 years, he made some extraordinary finds. He crossed the Kalahari Desert in southern Africa and discovered Lake Ngami. Livingstone believed that if a route could be found from either coast to central Africa, people would come from outside to trade.

With only a few African servants, Livingstone travelled by canoe, on ox-back and on foot, half-way across Africa to the west and then the whole way back from Loanda to Quelimane. He went where no European had ever been. He mapped the River Zambezi and named the Victoria Falls (known by Africans as 'smoke that thunders').

James Bruce of Kinnaird

Bruce (1730–94) (below) was a sickly child who became a dashing, red-haired giant of a man. Consumed with grief at the early death of his wife, he went to Africa, having first proposed marriage to a 16-year-old Stirlingshire girl, who promised to wait for him. He met her by chance in Florence on his way back 12 years later. She had married an Italian marquis. Bruce challenged him to a duel, but settled for an apology. His 3000-page *Travels to Discover the Source of the Nile* was published in 1790, although he was branded by some as a liar. His death was far less dramatic. Falling downstairs at his home, he died of his injuries.

Known as the Bruce Nile cup, this unusual object (left) includes the coconut shell used by Bruce of Kinnaird to toast the health of his monarch, King George III at Lake Tana, Ethiopia, on 4 November 1770.

David Livingstone

Livingstone was born at Blantyre, south of Glasgow, in 1813. At age ten, he started work in a cotton mill, but continued his education in the evenings. Aspiring to be a missionary doctor, in 1840 he gained a medical degree at Glasgow University. Enrolling in the London Missionary Society, he took up a post in Kuruman in southern Africa, in a mission run by Robert Moffat, marrying his daughter in 1845. After 32 years of exploration and campaigning against slavery in Africa, Livingstone died in 1873. His followers carried his body hundreds of miles to Zanzibar, for return to Britain and burial in Westminster Abbey.

Soon afterwards, the British Government invited Livingstone to lead an expedition to explore the Zambezi further. Though he and his Scottish chief assistant and naturalist, **John Kirk** (1832–1922) discovered Lake Shirwa and claimed to be the first to record the position and shape of Lake Nyasa, the expedition was a troubled one. After being recalled to Britain after six years, Livingstone sailed his purpose-built, collapsible river steam-boat across the Indian Ocean to Bombay, where he hoped to sell it.

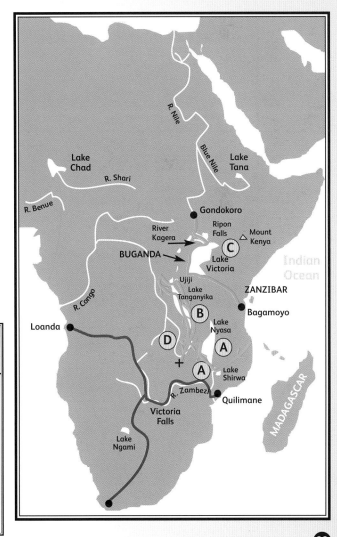

SCOTTISH EXPLORERS IN SOUTHERN, CENTRAL, AND EASTERN AFRICA

Livingstone's Great Journey	1858–64
Livingstone's Last Journey	1866–73
Grant (with Speke)	1860–62

A.   Regions explored by Livingstone and Kirk 1858–64
B.   Region explored by Thomson 1879–80 (see page 25)
C.   Region explored by Thomson 1883–84
D.   Region explored by Thomson 1890–91
+   Livingstone died here

Two years later, in 1866, **Livingstone** was on the trail again, this time to explore the waterways of Central Africa.

'Dr Livingstone, I presume?'

These famous words are thought to have been spoken in 1871 by Welsh-born journalist, Henry Morton Stanley. He had been sent by his American newspaper to find Livingstone, who was feared dead. After almost five years of travel Livingstone was stranded at Ujiji, after his stores had been stolen. Stanley gave him supplies and help, but Livingstone refused to accompany him back to Britain, saying that he still had work to do.

In 1873, desperately ill in the heat and torrential rains, Livingstone headed by mistake into a vast swamp. It took three months to get through it. Shortly afterwards, he died.

As a missionary, Livingstone made only one conversion to Christianity. His campaign, however, to eradicate the Arab slave trade in East Africa caused the British Government to take action.

In 1873, John Kirk, now consul in Zanzibar, was able to persuade the Sultan of Zanzibar to close down the trade in his region.

In the meantime, an expedition, led by **John Speke**, an Englishman, aided by the Scot **James Grant**, had in 1860 set out from Bagamoyo on the east coast to walk to Gondokoro, a trading post on the Nile. Their aim was to confirm Speke's disputed theory that Lake Victoria, which he had discovered in 1858, was the Nile's source.

In Buganda they learned of a great river that flowed out of Lake Victoria to the north. Grant was not with Speke when the latter discovered what he named Ripon Falls, which he believed to be the source of the Nile. As there was no one to confirm the find, it lead to a lot of controversy for many years.

Grant (left) with Speke, during their travels.

Mutesa, the king of Buganda, on the northern shores of Lake Victoria, holds a levee or assembly. Speke and Grant were the first Europeans to meet this tyrannical ruler, and spent some time at his court.

Speke and Grant had hoped to float down river to Gondokoro, but there were so many cataracts that they had to go on foot. The full journey had lasted almost two-and-a-half years.

Stanley's proof

It was in fact Henry Morton Stanley who, by sailing round Lake Victoria in 1875, finally proved that Speke and Grant were right about the Nile flowing out of it, and that River Kagera, which they had also discovered, was a major feeder into the lake.

In 1879 a Royal Geographical Society expedition assembled at Zanzibar to explore a possible trade route between the coast and lakes Nyasa and Tanganyika.

Its leader was **Keith Johnston** the younger (right), a map publisher and cartographer from Scotland. Shortly after the start, Johnston contracted severe dysentery and died.

Twenty-one-year-old **Joseph Thomson**, also Scottish, the expedition's geologist and naturalist, found himself in charge. In 1883 Thomson, the first European to walk from Mombasa to Lake Victoria, discovered the spectacular, 74-metre Thomson's Falls east of Mount Kenya. On the same expedition, he shot a gazelle – the species is now known as Thomson's gazelle or 'tommie'. Shortly before his death at the early age of 37, he wrote, 'I am doomed to be a wanderer. I am not an empire builder. I am not a missionary. I am not truly a scientist. I merely want to return to Africa and continue my wanderings.'

Thomson more than completed the expedition's assignment. In spite of chronic illness, he went on to lead, from the front, five further African explorations. In 15,000 gruelling miles, Thomson climbed several mountains, calmed various groups of hostile warriors, demonstrated the accessibility of the main East African lakes, and added much to the world's knowledge of the people and geography of East Africa.

Australia

How Scots colonists, with courage and determination, helped to develop a new land.

In 1800, in the survey ship, HMS *The Lady Nelson*, the Scot **James Grant** became the first commander to sail from west to east through the Bass Strait.

Somerset

Cape York Peninsula — (H)

Darwin

Arnhem Land

Gulf of Carpentaria

Kimberley

Ord River

King Leopold Ranges

NORTHERN TERRITORY

Central Mount Stuart

Lake Mackay

Macdonnell and Fergusson Ranges

(K)

WESTERN AUSTRALIA

1874

1869

(B)

Perth

Esperance

(K)

(K)

(I)

Simpson Desert

Barcoo River

Cooper Creek

SOUTH AUSTRALIA

Lake Eyre

1870

Lake Victoria

Adelaide

(C)

(D)

(C)

Murray River

VICTORIA

Glengower

Melbourne

Bass Strait

TASMANIA

(E)

(J)

QUEENSLAND

(H)

Bowen

Rockhampton

Warrego River

NEW SOUTH WALES

(F)

Darling River

(F)

(A)

Murrumbidgee R.

(C)

Sydney

(F) (G)

N
E ← → W
S

300 miles

SCOTTISH EXPLORERS OF AUSTRALIA

Stuart	1861	A.	Grant	1800, 1801
		B.	Stirling	1827
Landsborough	1861–62	C.	Sturt	
			and Macleay	1829
McKinlay	1861–62	D.	Cadell	1853
		E.	McKay	from 1835
J. and A. Forrest	1869, 1870	F.	Mitchell	1831–35
	and 1874	G.	McMillan	1864
		H.	Jardines	1864
A. and M. Forrest	1879	I.	Ross	1871
		J.	Dalrymple	
			and Johnstone	1873
		K.	Lindsay	1883–92

The next year Grant explored Hunter Valley as leader of an expedition which included as botanist **William Paterson**, an army officer who was also lieutenant-governor of New South Wales.

In 1827, HMS *Success* was sent to find a suitable site for settlement on the west coast. The ship's captain was **James Stirling**, with **Charles Frazer**, botanist to New South Wales, as scientific adviser. Point Belches is named after **Peter Belches**, one of the 18-man team that explored the Swan River.

Charles Sturt, with **George Macleay**, three soldiers, and three convicts, set out from Sydney in 1829 to explore the river system inland. They carried with them, in sections, a 7.5-metre whaling boat, which they launched in Murrumbidgee River in unknown territory. After a few days, they joined a broad river, which Sturt named Murray. He concluded that another river, flowing from the north, was the Darling. The outlet farther downstream, connecting Lake Victoria with the Murray, he called Rufus River after Macleay's shock of red hair. A fortnight later, having twice evaded threats from hostile Aboriginals, they found themselves on the coast. The return journey of 900 miles, rowed against a strong current with the men nearly starving, took 53 days, but the mystery of the rivers had been solved.

Alexander McKay was convicted of robbery in 1823 in Glasgow, and transported to Tasmania for life. Though said to be violent and untrustworthy, he was pardoned in 1831. As a member of the survey department, he traced River Mersey to its source, explored the shores of Great Lake and Lake St Clair, and followed the course of Gordon River.

Thomas Mitchell, Surveyor-General of New South Wales, extensively explored the south-east region during four expeditions between 1831 and 1845. Though he failed to find a river which he believed ran north into the Gulf of Carpentaria, he discovered the Warrego and Barcoo rivers, and the rich pasture land of central Queensland. He led an adventurous life in other respects too. In 1840, he was arrested in London for debt, and in 1851 he fought one of the last duels in Australia. Each man fired three shots, but both survived.

Francis Cadell

In 1853, Cadell (1822–79), in his purpose-built, flat-bottomed paddle steamer *Lady Augusta*, made the first successful steam voyage up the Murray, having previously examined the route downstream in a canvas boat. The riverside town of Cadell is named after him.

Fife-born **John McDouall Stuart** (1815–66) is regarded as Australia's finest inland explorer. He emigrated to South Australia in 1839.

In 1844 Stuart was a member of Sturt's expedition to the interior. Starting in 1858, Stuart led six expeditions north from Adelaide towards and beyond the central point of Australia. On 22 April 1860, he calculated that he was camped in the very centre of Australia. The next day he climbed the nearby mountain and built a cairn of stones, on which he raised the Union Jack (see right). He named the mountain Mount Sturt, after his first leader. It later became Mount Stuart.

In 1862, Stuart's ten-man team finally succeeded in crossing the entire continent from south to north, returning by the same route. The journey of 4250 miles was completed in one year. Of the 78 horses that started the expedition, only 42 survived.

On the return journey, Stuart's strength and eyesight failed after such punishing exertions over several years, and surveying duties were undertaken by 21-year-old **William Auld**. When Stuart could no longer support himself on his horse, a stretcher was constructed for him, hung on poles between two horses. In this way he was carried for 400 miles, as the sketch from memory (below) by a member of the expedition records.

the Party six
follow...
...about 40 pack-horses

Rough sketch to shew how J M Stuart was carried
on the ambulance from Mt Hay to Poster's Hill south of Chambers Creek in Dec
sketched from memory by Stephen King
(about 400 miles)
1862

Even so, the crossing of Australia had become a race, which Stuart had lost.

Robert O'Hara Burke and **William John Wills** had in 1861 reached the Gulf of Carpentaria by another route, only to disappear on the return journey. Three expeditions were set up immediately to find them, or their remains.

John McKinlay set out from Adelaide, while **William Landsborough** and his party were shipped to the Gulf to search from the north. The mystery was finally resolved when a sole survivor was found at Cooper Creek by **Alfred Howitt**, who had started from Melbourne. McKinlay and Landsborough continued their explorations and collected valuable information about the land and its climatic conditions. In the course of these, Landsborough made the first crossing of the continent from north to south, and McKinlay the third from south to north. The names of the towns Landsborough and McKinlay (Queensland) recall their exploits.

Search committee

In 1864, **Duncan McIntyre** announced that while exploring the route between Cooper Creek and the Gulf of Carpentaria he had found traces of Prussian explorer Friedrich Wilhelm Ludwig Leichhardt, lost in 1848. The Ladies' Leichhardt Search Committee funded McIntyre to lead an expedition. Its departure from Glengower, Victoria, is illustrated right. As nothing further was found, Leichhardt's disappearance remains a mystery.

Angus McMillan

Soon after his arrival in New South Wales in 1838, McMillan explored the plains of Gippsland. In 1864, aged 53, he was appointed leader of a government expedition to open up tracks in the mining areas east of where the Alpine National Park is today. When his team was disbanded (after 220 miles of track had been created through thick scrub), Mcmillan was determined to finish the job on his own, from Dargo to Moroka River. On the way, a pack-horse fell over on him — he died a few hours later at Iguana Creek.

In 1864, Scottish brothers **Francis** and **Alexander Jardine**, and eight others, left Rockhampton to drive stock of 42 horses and 250 cattle to their father's new posting at Somerset, Cape York Peninsula, 1200 miles away. Ten months later, dressed in rags and emu skin hats, they delivered 12 horses and 50 cattle. They had been through jungles and swamps, crossed broad rivers, and survived numerous Aboriginal attacks.

John Ross was, in 1871, among the second party to cross Australia from south to north through its centre. In 1870, he had led an advance exploration of a route for the overland telegraph, during which he made inroads into the Simpson Desert and discovered Todd River and the Fergusson Ranges.

George Dalrymple led an official expedition in 1873 north of Cardwell, then the most northerly port in Queensland. With him was **Robert Johnstone**, inspector of native police, after whom Johnstone River was named – he had discovered it earlier while investigating a massacre on Green Island.

John Forrest was 22 and brother **Alexander** 19, when in 1869, as expedition leaders, they searched from the west for traces of the lost explorer Leichhardt, covering over 2000 miles of unexplored territory. In 1870, with four other men and 16 horses, they were sent to blaze a trail from Perth to Adelaide. Having picked up supplies at Esperance, they became the first to cross Australia from west to east.

With an expedition of a similar size, the Forrest brothers set out in 1874 to explore the western centre of the continent. Despite difficulties in finding supplies of water for men and horses, and an attack by hostile Aboriginal people, they reached Peake's Telegraph Station, having crossed the desert which had previously deterred explorers who approached it from the east. The 11 out of 22 horses that survived the appalling conditions travelled the final leg of their journey to Adelaide in style, by train in horse-boxes.

John (mounted, right) and Alexander Forrest (left) sight the overland telegraph in 1874, signifying a milestone in Australian exploration. Alexander, with his younger brother Matthew and four others, went on in 1879 to explore the unknown region in the far north west, discovering and naming the district of Kimberley, King Leopold Ranges, and River Ord, with much rich pastureland besides.

John Forrest subsequently became Western Australia's first premier, and the first person born in Australia to be knighted.

Donald Mackay

Known as the 'last Australian explorer', **Donald Mackay** cycled 11,000 miles round Australia in 1889–1900 in the record time of 240 days, much of it through unknown territory. Between 1926 and 1928 he financed and took part in several expeditions in Northern Territory. Mackay's aerial surveys of central Australia during the 1930s revealed the vast lake which now bears his name.

Eccentric explorers

Accounts of travellers whose laid-back attitude enlivened the records of their explorations.

Most explorers were team leaders who enjoyed organisation, and valued the support and companionship of others. A few were loners, who preferred their own company and the challenges of solo exploration.

One such was **William Lithgow**, known as '**Lugless Will**' after his ears were cut off by the brothers of a girl he was courting. Between 1608 and 1627 Lithgow travelled, by his own account, 36,000 miles by sea and on foot, usually accompanied by a coffin. In this way, he explored much of Europe, the Mediterranean islands and the Middle East.

Lithgow was frequently attacked or captured. In Malaga, he was arrested as a suspected spy and, when he refused to confess, was tortured as a heretic by the Roman Catholic Church. Failing, on his return, to get compensation from Spain for his injuries, he assaulted the Spanish ambassador to London and was sent to prison. Lithgow described his travels as 'rare adventures and painful peregrinations'.

'Lugless Will'

Two centuries later, in the 1860s, **John MacGregor** made many solo journeys in canoes of his own design (all named *Rob Roy* after distant ancestor, Rob Roy MacGregor). In so doing, he turned canoeing into a popular British pastime. He paddled down the Rhine, Danube and other major European rivers, through Swiss lakes and in Scandinavia. Then, starting in Alexandria, he navigated the Suez Canal, Red Sea, River Jordan and Lake Gennesareth (Galilee). His travels were exciting, and his lively accounts of them were illustrated by himself.

John MacGregor

John MacGregor's book, *A Thousand Miles in a Rob Roy Canoe*, was published in 1866. Here, MacGregor describes his equipment and clothing:

'The Rob Roy Canoe was built of oak with a deck of cedar. ... My baggage for three months was in a black bag one foot square and six inches deep. A paddle seven feet long, with a blade at each end, and a lug sail and jib, were the means of propulsion; and a pretty blue silk Union Jack was the only ornament.

'My clothes consisted of a complete suit of grey flannel for use in the boat, and another suit of light but ordinary dress for shore work and Sundays. With [an] excellent new-fashioned coat and a Cambridge straw hat, canvas wading shoes, blue spectacles [and] a waterproof overcoat, there was sure to be a full day's enjoyment, defiance of rain and sun, deeps or shallows, hunger or *ennui* [boredom].'

Robert Louis Stevenson

Scottish author, **Robert Louis Stevenson**, took a trip through northern France and Belgium in a Rob Roy canoe named *Arethusa*.

He described it in *An Inland Voyage* (1878).

Isabella Bird wrote often and at length to her sister, Henrietta. One particular letter, sent from the Malay Peninsula in southeast Asia, was 116 pages long!

Isabella Bird was a Scottish resident from 1868 until her death in 1904. She married an Edinburgh doctor, John Bishop, when she was 49.

Bird was ill most of the time, except when travelling – the hard way. In Hawaii she climbed the world's highest volcano. She rode, astride and alone, over the Rocky Mountains, until she fell in – and possibly in love – with a Wild West desperado. She followed unknown tracks in northern Japan, Korea and Tibet, and at 60 she rode through heavy snow from Baghdad to Tehran, and visited remote tribes in south-west Persia. At 64, she journeyed 8000 miles in distant parts of China. Bird wrote popular books about her travels, and was the first woman fellow of the Royal Geographical Society.

Scientists and plantsmen

Scottish scientists and plantsmen (and women) who enhanced our knowledge of the world.

A wooden octant, dated *c*.1750. This scientific instrument was used to measure angular distances in navigation at sea.

Scientific instruments

A wooden octant was used to measure angles needed to work out a ship's position at sea. About 1758, **John Campbell**, having tested various instruments at sea, proposed that the instrument should be made of brass, and that its arc should be increased from 45 to 60 degrees. The new model, the sextant, revolutionised navigation and is the basis of the one used today.

Campbell had an eventful naval career as a master's mate and then master (navigator) on *Centurion*, flagship of George Anson's squadron, which set out on active duty against the Spanish in the eastern Pacific in 1740, and ended up sailing round the world. Of the six warships that began the voyage, only *Centurion* returned home, in 1744.

The *Challenger* expedition

This expedition was the idea of **Charles Wyville Thomson**. Its aim was to investigate the physics, chemistry, geology and biology of the world's oceans. The technical staff consisted of two other Scots, **John Murray** and **John Young Buchanan**.

The 70-metre corvette, fitted with a steam-driven propeller, spent 713 days at sea, and travelled 68,890 nautical miles. Soundings and temperature measurements were taken, and samples of bottom sediment, water and biological specimens were collected.

HMS *Challenger*

Not all explorers went in search of new lands, or to investigate the sea.

Some of Scotland's most famous explorers increased our knowledge of the natural world and improved our gardens, by bringing from abroad preserved birds, stuffed animals, seeds, live plants and trees.

Robert Brown (see page 16) failed to send back good seed to Edinburgh in 1863, but others were more successful. **Thomas Drummond** started work as a gardener at Doo Hillock, near Forfar. His skill drew the attention of **William Hooker**, Professor of Botany at the University of Glasgow, who recommended him to **John Richardson** as assistant (page 3).

In Canada, Drummond survived a terrible winter in a brushwood hut, without companions or books, and an attack by a grizzly bear. Back in North America in 1831, he sent to Hooker consignments of seeds, mosses, plants, reptiles (preserved in spirits), birds and insects. In 1835, a delighted Hooker received 3441 phlox seeds, which flowered brilliantly. In recognition of the discoverer, Hooker named the species, now common, *phlox Drummondii*. Later that year, three boxes arrived from Cuba, containing some of Drummond's belongings and a death certificate. It is not known how he died.

Like Thomas Drummond, **Robert Fortune** began life as a gardener. Trained at the Royal Botanic Garden in Edinburgh, he became, in 1842, the Horticultural Society of London's

Richardson's squirrel

During his time as naval surgeon with John Franklin's expeditions to the Arctic (page 3) and to Canada (1819–27), **John Richardson** observed many animals, fish, birds and plants. Later he contributed to *Fauna Borealis Americanae* (Latin: *Creatures of North America*), published between 1829 and 1837. Richardson's ground squirrel, from the grasslands of North America, is one of many biological specimens named after him. Others include Richardson's goose, salmon, aster, locowood, worm-wood and anemone.

Rhododendron fortunei (after Robert Fortune), photographed at Glendoick Gardens, near Perth.

collector in China. Here he learned Mandarin, shaved his head and wore a pigtail, survived violent storms on the Yellow Sea, was attacked by pirates on the Yangtze river and narrowly escaped falling into a trap full of wild pigs.

Fortune collected tea plants (sent to the Himalayas to start the Indian tea industry), roses, and peaches from the Emperor's garden. Later, visiting Japan, Fortune collected many plants that now grow in Scottish gardens. These include yellow jasmine, camellias, forsythia, tree peonies and the primula named *japonica*.

In the early 20th century, **Isabel Hutchison**, born at Kirkliston in 1899, became known as a traveller and plant collector. In 1924 she

In 1827, the Douglas fir, native to North America, was introduced to Scone Palace in Perthshire by **David Douglas**, who had worked there as a young gardener. Blind in one eye, dogged by illness and rheumatism, and prone to disastrous mishaps, Douglas nevertheless travelled widely in North America, sending back numerous live plants unknown in Europe. In Hawaii in 1834, he apparently fell into a pit-trap, and was gored to death by a wild bull. He was only 35.

walked across Iceland, and later travelled to Greenland, Alaska and, in 1937, its offshore Aleutian Islands. On these journeys she collected plants for the Royal Horticultural Society, and the Royal Botanic Gardens in Edinburgh and Kew. Some of the artefacts that she brought back are now in National Museums Scotland.

The Explorers' Garden

In Pitlochry you can visit a garden created to showcase 18 Scottish plant explorers. You can see a pavilion made from Douglas fir, and many of the plants and flowers brought back from faraway lands. Check out the website:

www.explorersgarden.com

At Scone Palace, near Perth, is a Pinetum holding a giant Douglas fir, raised from the first seed that David Douglas sent home from North America, and many other magnificent conifers. More information can be found at:

www.scone-palace.co.uk

Mountaineers

Some notable Scottish first ascents.

Frustrated that her husband was in the Scottish Mountaineering Club but she was not allowed to join, **Jane Inglis Clark** founded, with her daughter **Mabel** and a friend, **Lucy Smith**, the Ladies Scottish Climbing Club (LSCC), the first in Britain. Inaugurated in 1908, soon parties of women, dressed in long skirts, nailed boots and large hats, were seen on mountains over Scotland and beyond. **Lucy Smith** (left), with **Pauline Ranken** (below), honed her climbing skills on Salisbury Crags, Edinburgh.

In the late 19th and early 20th centuries, mountain tops, from the Scottish Highlands to the Himalayas, were among the most remote and unexplored places on earth. The 'Roof of the World' fascinated climbers looking for new heights to conquer.

Munro-bagging

The pastime of Munro-bagging originated with Sir Hugh Munro, who between 1889 and 1891 compiled a list of all Scottish summits of 3000 feet (914 metres) or more. There are 283, and they are known as Munros. At his death, Munro himself had climbed all but one. Today, more than 4000 people have completed the lot.

Although a small number of British mountaineers had climbed in the Alps, travel to distant lands was time-consuming and expensive, and many pioneering ascents took place in the Scottish Highlands. English climbers came north to the Cairngorms and Grampians, but many of the first ascents were made by members of the Scottish Mountaineering Club, founded in 1889 by a group of enthusiasts, and still flourishing.

An early recruit was **William Brown**, a young Edinburgh lawyer. With his climbing partner **William Tough** (who often cycled 40 miles from the nearest railway station before beginning to climb), Brown made the first ascent of the North Buttress (projecting cliff) of Buachaille Etive Mor. Later in the same year, 1895, the fearless pair made the first rock climb on Lochnagar, ascending a steep buttress now called the Tough-Brown Traverse.

At the end of the 19th century, other members of the SMC reached the summits of comparable Highland mountains. **William Naismith** and **William Douglas** followed Naismith's Route on Crowberry Ridge, Glen Coe in 1896; **John Hart Bell** scaled the Great Ridge, Garbh Bheinn in 1897, and in 1898, accompanied by **Harold Raeburn**, John Hart Bell climbed the Church-Door Buttress (so called by William Tough) in Glen Coe. Also in 1898, Harold Raeburn, accompanied by **William Inglis Clark** and **Jane Inglis Clark**, ascended Ben Nevis by the narrow, sharp-crested ridge known as Raeburn's Arête.

In the 20th century, as travel became faster and more convenient, British climbers began to venture further afield. By 1910, **Alexander Kellas** had taken part in first ascents of three Himalayan mountains – Sentinel Peak (6490 m), Pauhunri (7125 m) and Chomoyummo (6828 m). Others, both men and women, soon followed across the world.

Between 1934 and 1938, **Una May Cameron** was the first to climb Gara Chino (3858 m) and Simarchli (3850 m) in the Caucasus Mountains, and Neilion (5188 m) and Batian (5199 m) in Kenya. The towering Himalayas, along the northern border of India, presented the greatest challenge of all.

In 1955, three members of the LSCC – **Elizabeth Stark, Evelyn McNicol** and **Monica Jackson** – were first to climb Gyalgen Peak (6700 m). A year later (1956–58), **Tom Patey** was first to the top of Muztagh Tower (7273 m) and Rakaposhi (7788 m). Between 1970 and 1974, **Dougal Haston** conquered Annapurna South Face (7219 m) and Changabang (6864 m).

In 2009 a team from Glasgow Academy (4 leaders and 12 pupils, 3 of whom were girls), were first to climb the Greenland peak which they named Mount Glasgow (1820 m).

In his teens, Tom Patey (above) embarked on a series of first ascents in the Cairngorms, a practice which he continued in the Alps, Norway and the Himalayas. He is also credited with having founded sea-stack climbing in Scotland. He died in an abseiling accident, after the ascent of a sea-stack off the Sutherland coast.

Dougal Haston tackling Hillary Step, Everest, in 1975. He and Doug Scott, who took this photograph, were the first British mountaineers to reach the summit. Haston died at 36 in an avalanche, while skiing alone in the Alps.

Aviators

Some remarkable Scottish flights.

In 1784, James Tytler's hot air balloon lifted him 135 metres above Edinburgh.

EDINBURGH FIRE BALLOON

The first recorded attempt to fly in Scotland was short and unsuccessful. In 1507, **John Damien**, the Abbot of Tongland, tried to fly from the battlements of Stirling Castle, wearing a pair of wings he had made out of hen's feathers. Aiming for France, he landed ignominiously at the foot of the castle rock, and was lucky to escape with a broken leg. To his patron, King James IV, the Abbot blamed his choice of feathers: 'Hens,' he said, 'covet the middens and not the skies'. Almost four centuries would pass before the dream of flying with wings was achieved.

Meantime, another method was tested, and in the late 18th century, inspired by the successful hot air balloon flights of the Montgolfier brothers in France, Edinburgh-based **James Tytler** designed and constructed a similar balloon. On 27 August 1784, he flew from Abbeyhill to Restalrig – a British first in this type of flight. (As recently as 1990, Scotsman **Don Cameron** made a hot balloon flight from Britain to Russia.)

It was not until the very end of the 19th century that, as scientists' understanding of aerodynamics increased, flight with wings became possible. In 1897 **Percy Pilcher**, in a hang-glider, *The Hawk*, designed and built by himself in Scotland, broke the world

Percy Pilcher with his hang-glider, *The Hawk*, with his sister and assistant holding on. Pilcher was born in England of a Scottish mother, and was a member of the Naval Architecture Department, Glasgow University, from 1892 to 1896. This model was fitted with the world's first sprung-wheeled undercarriage. Pilcher died when it crashed during a demonstration in 1899.

Pilcher's Glider

record for such a machine with a flight of 250 metres. In the 1890s Pilcher had also been designing a powered aircraft which, after his death, experts decided was viable.

The first Scottish powered flight was made by **Harold Barnwell** in 1909. At their motor garage at Causewayhead, near Stirling, he and his brother **Frank** designed and constructed a biplane, powered by a Humber car engine. In it Harold flew 80 metres over Causewayhead, in the shadow of the Wallace Monument. Harold Barnwell was killed in a flying accident in 1917, but Frank, who had joined the Royal Flying Corps, headed a team of engineers who worked on combat aircraft towards the end of World War I.

It is astonishing how quickly aviation progressed after these early attempts. By 1919, a Scot, **Arthur Whitten Brown** was navigator to Englishman John Alcock in the first non-stop flight across the Atlantic. In the same year **Ross Macpherson Smith**, with his brother Keith as navigator, made the first flight from Britain to Australia, covering 11,340 miles in 135 flying hours.

King George V (fifth from the left) and Queen Mary (fourth from right) meet officials at the beginning of the England to Australia Air Race 1934. The couple (far right) are the pilots **Jim Mollison** and his wife, **Amy Johnson**, with, behind them, the De Havilland Comet in which they flew. They set a record of 22 hours for the leg from England to India, but failed to complete the course.

In 1931 another Scot, **Jim Mollison**, made the first solo flight from Australia to Britain, following this feat in 1932 by a solo flight across the Atlantic from east to west in 31 hours 20 minutes. This was the longest flight in a light plane, the first Atlantic crossing in such a machine, and the first from east to west.

In the pioneering years of aviation, recently emancipated women eagerly took to the skies; 16 Scots women, born between 1894 and 1915, received Aviators Certificates from the Royal Aero Club, founded in 1901. Of these **Janet Hendry** became the first Scottish woman pilot in 1928, and in 1933 **Winnie Drinkwater** became the first Scottish woman to pilot an airliner.

Winnie Drinkwater

Winnie Drinkwater, who in 1930 became Scotland's youngest pilot, is about to start the centre engine of a Midland & Scottish Air Ferries' biplane. In July 1933, in an open cockpit Fox Moth, she made the scheduled round trip from Renfrew to London and back.

RELATED WEBSITES

History of Navigation
www.abc.net.au/navigators/navigation/history.htm

Polar Regions – Scott Polar Research Institute – Historic Polar Images
www.freezeframe.ac.uk/home/home

The Fate of Franklin
www.ric.edu/faculty/rpotter/SJFranklin.html

Cool Antarctica
www.coolantarctica.com/index.html

Shackleton's voyage on the *Endurance*
www.pbs.org/wgbh/nova/shackleton/1914/

www.south-pole.com/homepage.html

Scott of the Antarctic – 1868 to 1912
www.solarnavigator.net/history/scott_of_the_antarctic_explorer_captain_robert_falcon.htm

'Doomed Expedition to the Pole, 1912': Eyewitness to History
www.eyewitnesstohistory.com/scott.htm

Canada

Dictionary of Canadian Biography Online
www.biographi.ca/index-e.html?PHPSESSID=lhhcgg31tv62lif9h8ujotf220

Passageways: True Tales of Adventure – for young explorers
www.collectionscanada.gc.ca/explorers/kids/index-e.html

Pathfinders and Passageways: The Exploration of Canada – for older explorers
www.collectionscanada.gc.ca/explorers/index-e.html

Africa

Livingstone Online – the medical writings of David Livingstone
www.livingstoneonline.ucl.ac.uk

Significant Scots: Hugh Clapperton
www.electricscotland.com/history/other/clapperton_ hugh.htm

Significant Scots: Mungo Park
www.electricscotland.com/history/other/park_mungo.htm

Australia

Australian Dictionary of Biography – Online Edition
www.adb.anu.edu.au

Australian Explorers
www.davidreilly.com/australian_explorers/

John McDouall Stuart – Surveyor-Explorer, 1815–66
johnmcdouallstuart.org.au/

Mountaineers

Scottish Mountaineering Club Pioneers
www.smc.org.uk/Gallery/SMC % 20Pioneers/menuindex.php

Ladies Scottish Climbing Club – brief history
www.ladiesscottishclimbingclub.org/index.php/history

Aeronauts

Captain Bertram Dickson
www.undiscoveredscotland.co.uk/usbiography/d/bertramdickson.html

Percy Sinclair Pilcher
www.ctie.monash.edu.au/hargrave/pilcher.html

Facts and activities section –

Page iv: **Word search** – The 20 words related to Scottish Explorers are highlighted in the box below.

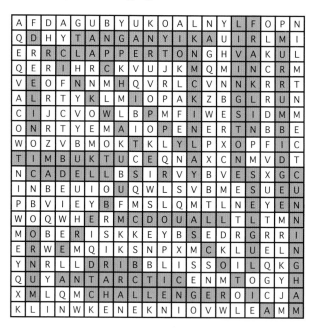

A	F	D	A	G	U	B	Y	U	K	O	A	L	N	Y	L	F	O	P	N
Q	D	H	Y	T	A	N	G	A	N	Y	I	K	A	U	I	R	L	M	I
E	R	R	C	L	A	P	P	E	R	T	O	N	G	H	V	A	K	U	L
Q	E	R	I	H	R	C	K	V	U	J	K	M	Q	M	I	N	C	R	M
V	E	O	F	N	N	M	H	Q	V	R	L	C	V	N	N	K	R	R	T
A	L	R	T	Y	K	L	M	I	O	P	A	K	Z	B	G	L	R	U	N
C	I	J	C	V	O	W	L	B	P	M	F	I	W	E	S	I	D	M	M
O	N	R	T	Y	E	M	A	I	O	P	E	N	E	R	T	N	B	B	E
W	O	Z	V	B	M	O	K	T	K	L	Y	L	P	X	O	P	F	I	C
T	I	M	B	U	K	T	U	C	E	Q	N	A	X	C	N	M	V	D	T
N	C	A	D	E	L	L	B	S	I	R	V	Y	B	V	E	S	X	G	C
I	N	B	E	U	I	O	U	Q	W	L	S	V	B	M	E	S	U	E	U
P	B	V	I	E	Y	B	F	M	S	L	Q	M	T	L	N	E	Y	E	N
W	O	Q	W	H	E	R	M	C	D	O	U	A	L	L	T	L	T	M	N
M	O	B	E	R	I	S	K	K	E	Y	B	S	E	D	R	G	R	R	I
E	R	W	E	M	Q	I	K	S	N	P	X	M	C	K	L	U	E	L	N
Y	N	R	L	L	D	R	I	B	B	L	I	S	S	O	I	L	Q	K	G
Q	U	Y	A	N	T	A	R	C	T	I	C	E	N	M	T	O	G	Y	H
X	M	L	Q	M	C	H	A	L	L	E	N	G	E	R	O	I	C	J	A
K	L	I	N	W	K	E	N	E	K	N	I	O	V	W	L	E	A	M	M

Scottish Explorers
Facts and activities

*'If you have men who will only come
if there is a good road, I don't want
them. I want men who will come if
there is no road at all …'*

David Livingstone (1813–73)

Latitude and longitude

The earth is round, like a sphere. How do we know where we are on its surface, and how do we describe our position?

Position is expressed by coordinates, measured in **degrees** (°) and **minutes** ('). The measurement represents the angle of a particular location, calculated from the centre of the earth.

Example 1

A coordinate in geography is a set of numbers and letters which indicate a position in terms of its latitude or longitude.

Edinburgh	55° 57' N (latitude)
	3° 12' W (longitude)
Glasgow	55° 52' N 4° 14' W
Aberdeen	57° 9' N 2° 6' W
London	51° 30' N 0° 5' W

For very precise measurement, a minute can be divided into 60 seconds ("), for example, 55° 52' 2".

The imaginary sphere which is the earth spins on an axis, the ends of which are the North and the South Pole. The Equator is a line right round the earth, at an equal distance from each of the poles. Its latitude is 0 degrees, and this is the starting point for measuring degrees of latitude. The line connecting all locations with the same latitude is called a line of latitude, or a parallel, since all lines of latitude are parallel to the Equator. There are 90 degrees of latitude running round the earth to the north of the Equator, and 90 degrees to the south.

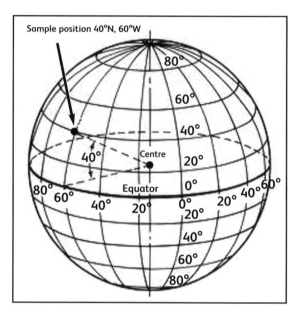

Sample position 40°N, 60°W

Example 2

Edinburgh is latitude 55 degrees 57 minutes north of the Equator: Glasgow is 55 degrees 52 minutes north (almost the same as Edinburgh); Aberdeen is 57 degrees 9 minutes north. A degree represents about 69 miles on the map, a minute about 1.15 miles.

Lines of latitude run horizontally round the earth. Lines of longitude, called meridians, run vertically, each of them passing through both poles. Lines of longitude are measured to the east or west of their 0 degree point, which by international agreement is the line which passes through Greenwich, UK. There are 180 degrees of longitude to the west of this line, and 180 degrees to the east. A degree of longitude varies in size, from about 69 miles at the equator, decreasing gradually to zero as the lines converge at one or the other of the poles.

Make your own compass

In the northern hemisphere a compass needle always points to the North Magnetic Pole. From this you can work out in which direction you are travelling, or, by placing a compass on a map, the direction you need to go to arrive at a certain point.

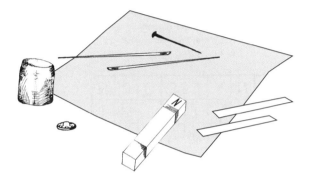

You will need:

– A piece of light card or stiff paper
– Two darning needles about 5 cm long
– One snap dress fastener
– One large pin
– A pair of compasses for drawing a circle
– A cork
– Tape, sticky on one side
– Pen/pencil
– Scissors
– A bar magnet

Method:

1. Magnetise each of the darning needles by stroking them gently in the same direction with one end of the bar magnet. (You may need to stroke each up to 20 times or more.)

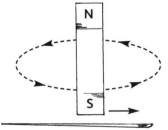

2. Use your pair of compasses to mark a disc of about 6 cm diameter in the piece of card. Cut it out. Write on it the points of the compass – **N**orth, **S**outh, **E**ast and **W**est.

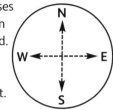

3. Make a hole in the centre of the card disc. Open the snap fastener and fix it together again from each side of the hole, with the hollow side of the fastener underneath.

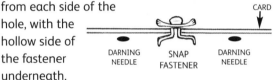

4. Fix the magnetised needles with the tape onto the underside of the disc each side of the snap fastener, with the ends towards which you have been stroking pointing in the same direction as **N** on the other side of the disc.

5. Make a base for your compass by pushing the pin through the cork so that it stands point upwards.

6. Balance the snap fastener of the disc on the point of the pin so that the disc is level, and can rotate freely. If the disc leans over to one side, you can improve the balance by sticking a small piece of the tape on the other side. [Note: some snap fasteners have a hole at the head through which the pin can slip. In this case cover the hole with sticky tape.]

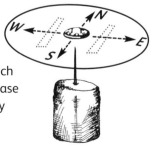

NB: Darning needles and pins are very sharp. Take great care when pushing the pin through the cork.

Word search

There are 20 words hidden in this word square that are related to Scottish Explorers. Can you find them?

Answers on page 40

ANTARCTIC	EREBUS	NILE
BIRD	FRANKLIN	SCOTIA
CADELL	LIVINGSTONE	TIMBUKTU
CHALLENGER	LUGLESS	TANGANYIKA
CHIPPY	MCDOUALL	
CLAPPERTON	MCKINLAY	
CUNNINGHAM	MUNRO	You can move diagonally, as well
DRINKWATER	MURRUMBIDGEE	as up and down, in any direction, to find the listed words.

A	F	D	A	G	U	B	Y	U	K	O	A	L	N	Y	L	F	O	P	N
Q	D	H	Y	T	A	N	G	A	N	Y	I	K	A	U	I	R	L	M	I
E	R	R	C	L	A	P	P	E	R	T	O	N	G	H	V	A	K	U	L
Q	E	R	I	H	R	C	K	V	U	J	K	M	Q	M	I	N	C	R	M
V	E	O	F	N	N	M	H	Q	V	R	L	C	V	N	N	K	R	R	T
A	L	R	T	Y	K	L	M	I	O	P	A	K	Z	B	G	L	R	U	N
C	I	J	C	V	O	W	L	B	P	M	F	I	W	E	S	I	D	M	M
O	N	R	T	Y	E	M	A	I	O	P	E	N	E	R	T	N	B	B	E
W	O	Z	V	B	M	O	K	T	K	L	Y	L	P	X	O	P	F	I	C
T	I	M	B	U	K	T	U	C	E	Q	N	A	X	C	N	M	V	D	T
N	C	A	D	E	L	L	B	S	I	R	V	Y	B	V	E	S	X	G	C
I	N	B	E	U	I	O	U	Q	W	L	S	V	B	M	E	S	U	E	U
P	B	V	I	E	Y	B	F	M	S	L	Q	M	T	L	N	E	Y	E	N
W	O	Q	W	H	E	R	M	C	D	O	U	A	L	L	T	L	T	M	N
M	O	B	E	R	I	S	K	K	E	Y	B	S	E	D	R	G	R	R	I
E	R	W	E	M	Q	I	K	S	N	P	X	M	C	K	L	U	E	L	N
Y	N	R	L	L	D	R	I	B	B	L	I	S	S	O	I	L	Q	K	G
Q	U	Y	A	N	T	A	R	C	T	I	C	E	N	M	T	O	G	Y	H
X	M	L	Q	M	C	H	A	L	L	E	N	G	E	R	O	I	C	J	A
K	L	I	N	W	K	E	N	E	K	N	I	O	V	W	L	E	A	M	M

Flight in Scotland

1784 **James Tytler**, in a hot-air balloon, makes the first British flight, from Abbeyhill to Restalrig, Edinburgh.

1897 **Percy Pilcher**'s hang-glider, *The Hawk*, designed and built by Pilcher in Scotland, breaks the world record for such a machine , flying to 250 metres.

1909 **Harold Barnwell**, at Causewayhead, Stirling, makes the first Scottish powered flight, in a biplane designed by himself and his brother **Frank**.

1910 **Captain Bertram Dickson** makes the first military aerial reconnaissance.

1919 **Arthur Whitten Brown**, as navigator, with Englishman **John Alcock** as pilot, make the first nonstop flight across the Atlantic in 16 hours 12 minutes. The next successful crossing was in 1927.

1919 **Ross Macpherson Smith**, with his brother Keith as navigator, and two engineers, make the first flight from Britain to Australia, covering 11,340 miles in 135 flying hours.

1923 **Norman Macmillan** is the first to fly nonstop from London to Sweden.

1928 **Janet Hendry** becomes the first Scottish woman pilot.

1931/2 **Jim Mollison** makes the first solo flight from Australia to Britain, in 8 days 19 hours. A year later he flies solo across the Atlantic from east to west in 31 hours 20 minutes: the longest flight in a light plane, the first Atlantic crossing in such a machine, and the first from east to west.

1933 **Lord Clydesdale** (**Douglas Douglas-Hamilton**) and **David Macintyre** are first pilots to fly over Mount Everest.

1933 **Winnie Drinkwater** is the first Scottish woman airline pilot.

1940 **Air Chief Marshal Sir Hugh Dowding** is chief of Fighter Command during the Battle of Britain.

1940 **Squadron Leader Archie McKellar** DSO (posthumous), DFC and bar, dies in action, having personally shot down at least 17 enemy aircraft in the previous 11 months.

1945 **Marion Wilberforce** leaves Air Transport Auxiliary, having since 1940 flown over 100 different kinds of aircraft, including four-engine bombers.

1946 Marshal of the Royal Air Force **Sir Arthur Tedder** is appointed chief of the air staff, having in 1944 been deputy commander of the allied invasion of Europe.

1972 **Don Cameron** flies over the Alps in the largest hot-air balloon ever built.

1990 **Cameron** makes the first balloon flight from Britain to USSR.

For more information about this subject, see the Scottie book, *Flight in Scotland*.

Scottish explorers

Scottish scientists whose explorations have enhanced our knowledge of the world.

Dates indicate the years between which the subject was actively engaged in exploration.

Biologists

James Murray (1907–14): Antarctic, Arctic (see pp. 7 and 10)

Robert Clark (1914–17): Antarctic

James Marr (1920–45): Antarctic, Arctic

Botanists and plant collectors

Francis Masson (1772–1805): southern Africa, West Indies, Portugal, Madeira, Canada

Thomas Blaikie (1775): Swiss Alps

William Paterson (1777–1801): southern Africa, eastern and western Australia (see p. 27)

Alexander Anderson (c.1780–1811): West Indies

John Fraser (c.1784–1809): North America, Cuba

Archibald Menzies (1786–1801): North America, south-western Australia, Sandwich Islands, West Indies

Charles Frazer (1817–27): eastern and western Australia (see p. 27)

George Don jnr (1821–23): Sierra Leone, Madeira, West Indies, Brazil

David Douglas (1823–34): North America, Sandwich Islands

Thomas Drummond (1825–35): North America

James Drummond (1836–c.60): western Australia

Thomas Thomson (1841–51): Afghanistan, Himalayas, Tibet, Kashmir, India

David Lyall (1841–61): Arctic, Antarctic, New Zealand, North America

Robert Fortune (1843–53): China, Java, Taiwan, Japan

John Jeffrey (1850–54): Canada

Robert Brown (1863–66): Vancouver Island (see p. 16)

George Forrest (1904–32): south-western China

Isabel Hutchison (1924–37): Iceland, Greenland, Alaska, northern Canada, Aleutian Islands

George Sherriff (1933–49): Tibet, Bhutan, northern India

Cartographers

James Mackay (1791–97): Missouri River (North America)

Keith Johnston (1873–79): Paraguay, East Africa (see p. 25)

Geologists

William Logan (1843–63): Canadian Geological Survey

Alexander Murray (1843–80): Canada West, Newfoundland

James Richardson (1846–71): Canada

James Hector (1857–65): western Canada, New Zealand

Thomas Macfarlane (1863–68): Lower and Upper Canada

Henry Drummond (1879–84): Rocky Mountains (Canada), East Africa

James Wordie (1914–47): Antarctic, Arctic (p. 12)

Hydrographer

Alexander Dalrymple (1759–64) (right): East Indies

Naturalists

Andrew Graham (1767–75): Hudson's Bay
(Canada)

John Richardson (1819–49): Arctic, Canada

John MacGillivray (1842–55): Australian east
coast, south-west Pacific

William Speirs Bruce (1896–1904): Arctic,
Antarctic (see p. 9)

Navigators

John Campbell (1756–86): Trials at sea of
navigational instruments

James Weddell (1819–24): Antarctic (see p. 8)

Oceanographers

John Murray (1868–1911): Arctic, *Challenger*
expedition, Faroe

Charles Wyville Thomson (1868–76):
Mediterranean, *Challenger* expedition

John Young Buchanan (1872–86): *Challenger*
expedition, South America, Africa

Some notable Scottish mountaineers

First ascents

1895   William Brown – Tough-Brown Traverse,
Lochnagar

1896   William Naismith, William Douglas –
Naismith's Route, Crowberry Ridge,
Glencoe

1897   John Hart Bell – Great Ridge, Garbh
Bheinn

1897   J. Norman Collie – Mount Victoria
(3464 m), Rocky Mountains, Canada

1898   John Hart Bell, Harold Raeburn – Flake
Route, Church-Door Buttress, Glen Coe

1901   Rev. Archibald Robertson – all Munros
completed

1902   William Inglis Clark, Jane Inglis Clark,
Harold Raeburn – Raeburn's Arête, Ben
Nevis

1902   J. Norman Collie – Mount Forbes
(3612 m), Rocky Mountains, Canada

1910   Alexander Kellas – Sentinel Peak
(6490 m), Pauhunri (7125 m), and
Chomoyummo (6828 m), Himalayas

1911   J. Norman Collie – Barricade Mountain
(3112 m), Rocky Mountains, Canada

1920   Harold Raeburn: winter ascent,
Observatory Ridge, Ben Nevis

1929   George Graham Macphee – Route 1,
Ben Nevis

1932   Una May Cameron – Gora Chino
(3858 m) and Simarchli (3850 m),
Tschauchee Group, Caucasus

1933   Thomas Brown – Mont Blanc (4810 m)
by six separate routes

1936   George Graham Macphee – South
Gully, Ben Nevis (solo)

1938   Una May Cameron – Nelion (5188 m)
and Batian (5199 m), Kenya (first by a
woman)

1940   J. H. B. Bell – Long Climb, Orion Face,
Ben Nevis

1955   Ladies Scottish Climbing Club
(Elizabeth Stark, Evelyn McNicol,
Monica Jackson) – Gyalgen Peak
(6700 m), Himalayas

1956   Tom Patey – Muztagh Tower (7273 m),
Himalayas

1958   Tom Patey – Rakaposhi (7788 m),
Himalayas

1970   Dougal Haston – Annapurna South
Face (7219 m), Himalayas

1974   Dougal Haston – Changabang
(6864 m), Himalayas

c.1975 Alistair McKeith – Tatakakken Falls,
Canada (ice climb)

PLACES OF INTEREST

Listed below are a number of places in Scotland associated with Scottish Explorers. For additional information, contact local Tourist Information offices.

SCOTLAND

Blantyre: The David Livingstone Centre
165 Station Road, Blantyre G72 9BY
www.nts.org.uk/property/David-Livingstone-Centre

Dundee: Discovery Point
Discovery Quay, Dundee DD1 4XA
www.rrsdiscovery.com/index.php?pageID=129

Edinburgh: National Museum of Scotland
Chambers Street, Edinburgh EH1 1JF
www.nms.ac.uk

Royal Botanic Garden Edinburgh
20A Inverleith Row, Edinburgh EH3 5LR

(see also **Royal Botanic Garden** in **Benmore, Argyll, Dawyck** in the **Scottish Borders** and **Logan** in **Dumfries and Galloway**)
www.rbge.org.uk

Pitlochry: Explorers Garden
Port-na-Craig, Pitlochry PH16 5DR
www.explorersgarden.com

ENGLAND

London: Natural History Museum
Cromwell Road, London SW7 5BD
www.nhm.ac.uk

Richmond, Surrey: Royal Botanic Garden
Kew, Richmond, Surrey TW9 3AB
www.kew.org/

FURTHER CREDITS

OTHER TITLES IN THE SCOTTIES SERIES
(eds Frances and Gordon Jarvie)

The Clans (Gordon Jarvie)
The Covenanters (Claire Watts)
Flight in Scotland (Frances and Gordon Jarvie)
Greyfriars Bobby: A Tale of Victorian Edinburgh (Frances and Gordon Jarvie)
The Jacobites (Antony Kamm)
Mary, Queen of Scots (Elizabeth Douglas)
The Romans in Scotland (Frances Jarvie)
Robert Burns in Time and Place (Frances and Gordon Jarvie)
Scotland's Vikings (Frances and Gordon Jarvie)
Scottish Rocks and Fossils (Alan and Moira McKirdy)
Scottish Kings and Queens (Elizabeth Douglas)
Supernatural Scotland (Eileen Dunlop)
There shall be a Scottish Parliament (Frances and Gordon Jarvie)